# SUMMER

## DISCOVERING THE SEASONS

*Written by Louis Santrey*

*Photography by Francene Sabin*

**Troll Associates**

*Library of Congress Cataloging in Publication Data*

Santrey, Louis.
  Summer.

  (Discovering the seasons)
  Summary: Text and photographs describe weather
conditions, plant growth, and animal behavior that
occur between spring and fall.
  1. Summer—Juvenile literature.   2. Seasons—
Juvenile literature.   [1. Summer.   2. Seasons] I. Sabin,
Francene, ill.   II. Title.   III. Series: Santrey, Louis.
Discovering the seasons.
QB631.S258   1983        508        82-19384
ISBN 0-89375-911-2 (case)
ISBN 0-89375-912-0 (pbk.)

*For their special photo contributions, the publisher
wishes to thank: Janice Lozano, pages 15 (right), 17;
Melody Norsgaard-Ashe, pages 18, 24 (left), 30
(bottom); Colour Library International, pages 3, 4,
32; H. Lanks/FPG, page 30 (top).*

Printed in the United States of America

10    9    8    7    6    5    4    3

It is a perfect afternoon. Under a cloudless sky, a butterfly flutters from one flower to another, sipping nectar. The air is hot, and it is so quiet and peaceful that the whole world seems to be asleep. Today is the longest day of the year. It is the first day of summer.

Summer. It is a time of sunshine and warmth. Forest and field are alive with color. Days are long, and nights are short. Summer is a time of plenty. It is a wonderful time for all living things.

Beautiful plants grow everywhere, in sunlight and in shade. Deep in the woods, under an umbrella of trees, it is dark and damp. Here, Nature's feathers of the forest—the ferns—wave their delicate green plumes. The fern is one of Earth's oldest plants. Fossils show that relatives of today's fern grew hundreds of millions of years ago.

The hardy wild rose will live just about anywhere the sun shines. Wild roses can grow in the shape of a bush or as a vine that wraps itself around the trunk of a tree. Called the "Queen of Flowers," the rose—with its silky petals and sweet aroma—is one of summer's prettiest blooms.

The hum and buzz of insects fills the warm summer air. Bees flit from flower to flower, collecting nectar to make honey. They live in hives with many other bees. Most wasps live alone. They build their nests and lay their eggs in plant stems, under the ground, or in rotting tree trunks.

The long, slender dragonfly, with its four see-through wings, is one of the fastest-flying insects. It is also one of the oldest insects on Earth. There were dragonflies one hundred fifty million years ago, during the very time that dinosaurs roamed the Earth.

The summer pond is bursting with life. Duckweed and cattails, reed grass and watercress, pondweed and water lettuce, spike rushes and saw grass—all push for room to grow. In the shallow water near shore, water lilies, with flat, heart-shaped leaves and yellow flowers, dot the top of the pond like small suns.

At the pond's edge, a young turtle hitches a piggy-back ride on a large old turtle. If danger should be near, turtles pull their heads and legs into the safety of their tough shells. The bullfrog squats in the water, watching for insects to fly near. Then *zap!* Its sticky tongue darts out and captures the insect.

The beauty of summer is seen best in its flowers.
Lovely blooms paint the land in a rainbow of
pretty colors. Their blossoms are like strings of tiny
bells, brightly colored snowballs, or a fireworks
display.

The day lily opens its orange-and-yellow petals in the morning and closes them when night falls. It lives for only one day, which is why it is called the day lily. The bright yellow sunflower stands tall in summer gardens. Birds, animals—and people— love to eat its seeds.

High in a maple tree is a blue jay's nest. There are eggs in it. At least one parent guards the nest and keeps the eggs warm until they hatch. Its gray and blue feathers make this bird hard to spot among the shadows. When the down-covered baby jay is three weeks old, it leaves the nest to find out about the world below.

13

A mother Muscovy duck struts about, all the while keeping a watchful eye on her little ones. The fluffy yellow ducklings follow her for a while, then begin to wander. She quickly herds them together, pushing and prodding them with her bill, quacking loudly at each one to "get back in line."

Summer is the season of plenty for animals of the forest and field—plenty of food, plenty of sunlight, and long, warm days. The forest animals—both large and small—eat all they can find. The shy chipmunk nibbles at a snip of grass, always ready to run for cover. A big bear lumbers about in search of insects and berries.

The blossoms are gone from the apple tree. In their place are hard, green young apples. Rain and sun will help them grow fat and juicy and sweet. Strawberries grow close to the ground. The tasty red fruit get ripe and ready for picking very fast—if the rabbits and birds don't eat them first.

Summer brings sunshine-filled days. Fluffy white clouds drift across the blue sky, like sailboats on a calm sea. At last, it is evening, and the sun begins to set. It is as if Nature is dimming the lights, while the daytime animals get ready for sleep.

The short summer night is soon over. At dawn, the birds and other animals begin to stir. Two cormorants perch in the branches of a tree near the lake. These long-necked birds dive deep into the water, seizing fish with their powerful beaks. Their webbed feet help them to swim.

Caterpillars are everywhere to be seen during the summer months. Although they are slow movers, caterpillars lead busy lives. They spend all day eating the soft green leaves of trees and shrubs. As they get larger, they outgrow their skins.

Four times a caterpillar sheds its old, tight skin, coming out bigger and more beautiful with each change. When the caterpillar has reached its full size, it spins a cocoon of silk around itself. It will stay in the cocoon until it is time to come out as a moth.

When the summer sun shines, up come the weeds. Two of these are the thistle and the wild carrot plant. The thistle grows wherever the soil is rich. Its leaves are thorny, but its purplish flowers are silky and soft. The wild carrot has flowers that look like fancy white lace—that's why this plant is also called Queen Anne's Lace.

Mushrooms and toadstools can usually be found growing on the damp, dark forest floor. Or they may spring up in the garden after a heavy rain. They come in all shapes and sizes. Some mushrooms look like bird baths, umbrellas, baseballs, rockets, or trumpets. These unusual plants do not have roots, flowers, or leaves. They can be white, red, brown, orange, and many other colors—but they are never green.

Some summer creatures move so-o-o slowly. Others dart about swiftly. One of the slowest is the slug. It is a snail without a shell on its back. The slug lives in damp places and leaves a sticky, silvery trail behind it. The speedy, insect-eating lizard can be very hard to see. It is able to stay very still, blending in perfectly with the plant it is clinging to.

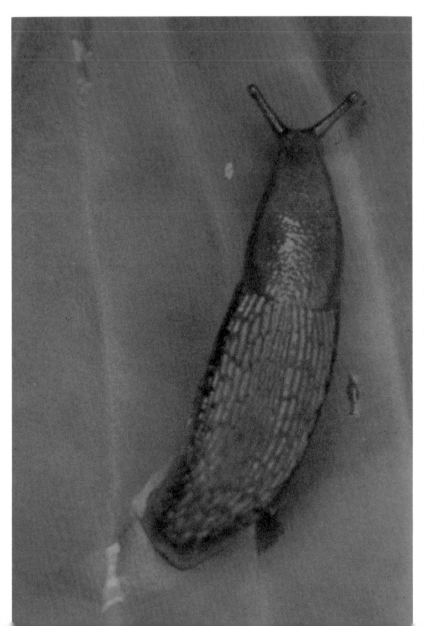

The green heron, the white egret, and the wood duck spend the summer months near ponds, marshes, and lakes. The heron and egret wade in shallow water, searching for a fish or a frog. When they see one, they scoop it up in a long bill and swallow it whole. The wood duck, also called the perching duck, has beautifully colored feathers of green, brown, black, and white.

In open fields, bathed in bright sunshine, wild-flowers grow in great numbers. They spring up wherever their seeds are blown by the winds or carried by the birds. The black-eyed Susan has petals as yellow as the sun itself, and a chocolate-brown center. The red clover isn't really red—it's pinkish-purple, and a favorite food of cattle.

Wildflowers are an important part of Nature. Insects sip their sugary nectar, and both animals and people eat the tender green leaves and blossoms of certain wildflowers. The chicory flower is pale blue, and its leaves are sometimes used in salads. The yellow goldenrod is seen growing everywhere—in swamps, in the woods, and even in many gardens.

The gentle fawn, born in the spring, grazes near its mother. It will not lose its spots until it is older. The adult male deer has a new crown of antlers with a velvety covering. These antlers have taken the place of the antlers that fell off last winter.

The sounds of insects fill the August air. All day, the grasshoppers "sing" a chirping, buzzing chorus. They make the sounds by rubbing a hind leg against a front wing. At night, the crickets begin their song. They "sing" by rubbing one front wing over the other front wing. Both insects eat grasses and seeds.

One of the most colorful of all butterflies is the
monarch, with wings like orange-and-gold stained
glass. A great wanderer, the monarch flies as far
north as Canada in the summer, and as far south as
Mexico in the winter.

The praying mantis gets its name from the way it stands. It stays very still, with both front legs close together, as if folded in prayer. But the mantis isn't praying; it is waiting for insects to come close. The praying mantis is helpful to people and plants because it eats many harmful insects.

In the last days of August, many plants stop making new leaves and blossoms. They grow pale and dry. Spring is many cold months ahead, but the plants will be ready when it comes. Right now they are sending out seeds. Next year, when winter ends, the seeds will become new grasses and flowers, bringing fresh color and a bright feeling to the world.

As autumn draws near, each day is a little bit shorter than the one before. Even at noon the sun does not ride as high in the sky. And when it sets, the air turns cool. But summer, the season of plenty, has given us many gifts. Days filled with sunshine, beautiful, bright flowers, and long, peaceful afternoons. All these, and more, have been the gifts of a glorious season—summer.